THE CHEATING BOYFRIEND

AND OTHER ORGANIZATIONAL INDISCRETIONS

JENNY HAYES, MSOD, PHR

THE CHEATING BOYFRIEND

And Other Organizational Indiscretions

JENNY HAYES, MSOD, PHR

Copyright © 2017 by Jenny Hayes

All rights reserved. This book or any portion thereof may not be reproduced or used in any manner whatsoever without the express written permission of the publisher except for the use of brief quotations in a book review.

Printed in the United States of America

First Printing, January 2017

Second Printing, May 2020

Third Printing, March 2025

Library of Congress Control Number: 2017902001

US Copyright Registration Number: TX0009438768

ISBN-13: 978-1-7367715-0-1 (hardcover)

ISBN-13: 978-1542646406 (paperback)

ISBN-13: 978-0-9986453-0-8 (ebook)

Blue Milk Publishing, San Jose, CA

bluemilk.co

DEDICATION

This book is dedicated to my dad, James Craig Hayes (1950-2017). Thank you for being a "useful manager!" We should all strive to manage personnel the way you did in your 35 years in the pizza business.

EDITORIAL REVIEWS

The Cheating Boyfriend (And Other Organizational Indiscretions)

"A wise and well-crafted little book about the nitty-gritty of organizational life, with lovely advice about how to keep your sanity and dignity intact."

— ROBERT SUTTON, PHD, STANFORD PROFESSOR AND AUTHOR OF *GOOD BOSS, BAD BOSS*

"A fun guide that you'll breeze through in a sitting. Hayes frequently peppers her workplace examples with pop culture references, which elevates the book above a dry managerial manual into something much more lively and entertaining."

— SELF-PUBLISHING REVIEW

PREFACE

A perfect organization does not exist. Behind closed doors, there are many "indiscretions" that take place. Over the years, I have encountered many organizational faux pas, but I don't think I truly appreciated this until I entered graduate school.

I began the University of San Francisco Master's in Organization Development (OD) program in 2011. In OD, you are asked often to self-reflect. Self-reflection really opened my eyes to organizational challenges and matured me as a business professional. I felt I should pay it forward and start blogging about my insights.

My first published article centered on organizations and management was "The Cheating Boyfriend." The leading recruiting news site, ERE.net, picked it up. The story went viral and became the top news story on LinkedIn!

But why "The Cheating Boyfriend," you ask? Well, it's an intriguing title, for starters. However, it's not meant to defame a gender. You can easily replace the word "boyfriend" with anyone in which you are in a romantic relationship. I felt that a relationship analogy would easily help people understand the concept of "cheating managers."

Since that post, I have written dozens of other stories that have been published in numerous business blogs and magazines. This book chronicles many of them. Most of what you will find are tongue-in-cheek analogies that express my personal observations on various matters in the business world. At the end the of day, I hope these stories will inspire you to not sit idle and make some positive organizational change!

Jenny Hayes, MSOD, PHR
January 2017

INDISCRETION #1

The Cheating Boyfriend Syndrome

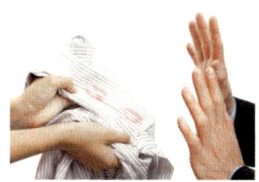

Back in college, I dated a guy who used to go out to clubs late at night (after he would stop by to see me). He would go to these clubs with one of his buddies and would be dancing with other girls. He would tell me, "Don't worry, Jenny. I tell them that I have a girlfriend." Sure. Needless to say, I ended that relationship after 5 months...

But, let's say that I didn't get out of that relationship. Let's say this behavior continued for years. He would lead me to believe that everything was fine with the relationship. However, he was out there meeting other girls, maybe having a side relationship with a random girl he met at a club. So, I just wasted years of my life with someone, and all the while he was having his cake and eating it, too.

In organizations, managers have been infamous for being "the cheating boyfriend." They string employees along who they know aren't an organizational fit but keep them around because of fear: fear of finding a replacement; fear of retaliation; fear of feeling guilty for letting someone go. It's time for managers to stop being the cheating boyfriend!

You are doing this person a disservice. Be an advisor. Be honest. In my experience as a manager, I make it very clear to people where I think they should fit. I once told one of my direct reports that she would have made an excellent office manager. I may have put an idea in her head, and maybe she'll leave to become an office manager — but, hey, I am not going to string people along. I'm not going to be the cheating boyfriend.

At the June 2005 Stanford University commencement, the late co-founder of Apple, Steve Jobs, stated: "Your work is going to fill a large part of your life, and the only way to be truly satisfied is to do what you believe is great work. And the only way to do great work is to love what you do. If you haven't found it yet, keep looking. Don't settle. As with all matters of the heart, you'll know when you find it. And, like any great relationship, it just gets better and better as the years roll on."

As an organization, we need to be hiring for fit. As a job seeker, we shouldn't settle. It's about passion. Passion will allow you to find the perfect match — your soul mate. No more cheaters!

INDISCRETION #2

Management's Minions

Imagine this: you are at your company's holiday party. Past and present employees are invited. The CEO decides to do an award ceremony. She honors various employees for their hard work. You sit there, patiently, hoping you will be recognized soon, as most people seem to be given an award, and you were just told the other day by the CEO that you were doing a great job.

It's towards the end of the ceremony. The CEO says she has one last award: she gives a round trip ticket around the world to your former boss who left the company 4 months ago. And, by the way, she gave him a $5,000 bonus on his last week of employment for some "project" that he worked on. You are left empty handed and with an undercooked steak for a meal...

Yes, crazy things like this go on in small business – it's called cronyism, and it's in abundance.

Good managers don't allow this in their organization. They have to be neutral and fair. Yes, it's natural that you become more affiliated with one person over another, but you are dealing with people's emotions.

In 2011, Georgetown University's McDonough School of Business conducted a survey in which senior business executives (92 percent) said they have seen favoritism at play in employee promotions, including at their own companies (84 percent)[1].

"It's impossible not to build friendships in an organization," Rachelle Bello, HR Director at RiseSmart, said. "The key is not to play favorites. Being objective demands respect – and respect is key in any relationship."

So how can individual contributors combat this? In the workplace, the number one, most important thing is the business at hand. You could quit and find a new job to make a statement. You can escalate the matter to a trusted leader, who may be well equipped to handle the situation. However, the best option, especially if you like your job overall, may just be to wait it out.

Author and activist Maya Angelou once said: "It is only out of ignorance that people are cruel, because they really don't think it will come back." In other words, don't let managerial minions crawl under your skin; in the end, it's just not worth it.

INDISCRETION #3

Fifty Shades of Management

I dated a guy for 4 months who travelled a lot for work. When we did get a chance to spend time together in person, we had incredible chemistry. Then, he had to move to Iowa because his mom was very ill. At first, he was okay with a long distance relationship, but then he felt that I became too controlling ("oppressive" was the word he chose). So, I asked him if we could at least still remain friends. He sternly said no. He told me that he was going to a "dark place" and that he didn't want to drag me down with him...

Yikes! That was pretty harsh; however, this relationship actually got me to thinking more about "control" and how that affects management styles. The biggest "control freak" that I have read about in recent times is none other than Christian Grey, from the *50 Shades* novels.

50 Shades of Grey and its sequels are the *Twilight*-inspired fan fiction novels that have sold over 100 million copies and have turned into a series of movies starring

Dakota Johnson and Jamie Dornan. The central character in the trilogy is the mysterious billionaire magnate, Christian Grey. He is a young and handsome Seattle entrepreneur with peculiar "tastes." He meets the recent college graduate Anastasia Steele, and the two begin a complicated love affair. Say what you will about the writing style of E.L. James, but, believe it or not, through the dialog, she provides some pretty accurate insights into the mind of the entrepreneur. Let's take a look at 5 of Mr. Grey's quotes, and let's see how they measure up to success in business today.

"I exercise control in all things, Miss Steele."

A few years ago, I took a Thematic Apperception Test (TAT). How the TAT works is that you are given some ambiguous photographic scenario, and you are to write a story based on the imagery. The results of my test were that of the entrepreneur: high need for achievement, low need for affiliation and very high need for control. I was fine with this analysis, but I was a bit concerned about the control part. For the entrepreneur (and anyone for that matter who exhibit a high need for control), one must caution the type of control one desires. Psychologist David McClelland[2] stated that the need for control could be a positive quality when it is about governing and fostering others and the organization as a whole (also known as "socialized power"). The need for control becomes dangerous when it's about commanding and oppressing. In the case of Christian Grey, it was a bit hard to tell initially what type of "control freak" he really was, but over the course of the novels, we learn that Christian does have a fostering side for his employees, especially for his assistant, Taylor.

> *"Business is all about people, Miss Steele, and I'm very good at judging people."*

Understanding those around you is critical when leading an organization. Making solid judgment calls can lead to anticipating problems before they happen - very important for entrepreneurs (and business in general). We look at both extrinsic (social status, job titles, appearance) and intrinsic qualities/values (attitude, will, stamina) when judging. Christian Grey, being a young man at age 27, is still relatively "green" by most business standards; however, he is able to maintain a hugely successful enterprise. In *The Wall Street Journal* article entitled "Judgment Trumps Experience[3]," the authors state that "wisely processed experience, reflection, valid sources of timely information, an openness to the unbidden and character are critical components of judgment." What Christian Grey does is take what he knows, even with his limited experience, and makes the best judgment calls based on intrinsic and extrinsic data collection.

> *"I employ an exceptional team, and I reward them well."*

Retaining talent is very difficult - especially if you are a start-up. Christian Grey built his enterprise from scratch, so he had to find ways to get top-talent to join him in his ambition. We hear about legendary perks from companies such as Google and Facebook. It would have been interesting to know what perks Mr. Grey provided his employees. There is a great *Mashable* article[4] that outlines some of the top perks given by start-ups. Wonder if, after 1 year of employment, you would get to ride in Charlie Tango?!

"My belief is to achieve success in any scheme one has to make oneself master of that scheme, know it inside and out, know every detail. I work hard, very hard to do that."

Going back to the need for control, Christian Grey never let any part of his business escape his radar. I think it's critical to be a hands-on manager and leader ... not to be a control freak but to be well informed about the business and how to take it to the next level. Like I mentioned in my article "5 Ways to Be a Useful Middle Manager[5]," you have to roll up your sleeves and dive deep with your team.

"I make decisions based on logic and facts. I have a natural gut instinct that can spot and nurture a good solid idea and good people."

It sounds a bit cold, but Christian Grey makes a good point about the natural gut instinct in solid decision-making. A recent *Forbes* article[6], neuroscience in business expert Janet Crawford states that "most neuroscientists would agree that well over 90% of our behavior is generated outside of consciousness. We are more slaves to our biology than we realize. Our rational minds represent a very small layer floating atop a vast well of unconscious drivers. Business leaders who understand biological programming and can leverage it possess an enormous advantage."

INDISCRETION #4

The Useless Middle Manager

"Hello, Peter. What's happening? Ummm, I'm gonna need you to go ahead and come in tomorrow. So, if you could be here around 9 that would be great, mmmk... Oh, oh - and I almost forgot; ahh, I'm also gonna need you to go ahead and come in on Sunday, too, 'kay. We, ahh, lost some people this week and, ah, we sorta need to play catch up..."
- Bill Lumbergh

Uh, yeah....that's the portrait of the classic floating head middle manager that we found in the movie *Office Space* ... the kind of boss we dreaded; someone we would never respect and hope would vanish into thin air. Believe it or not, according to *The Wall Street Journal*[7], there are over 10.8 million potential "Lumberghs" running amuck in corporate America. If you are one of these 10.8 million, there is hope for you! Here are 5 ways to break free of the vicious cycle and become useful:

1. Roll Up Your Sleeves

One thing that will command respect from your direct reports is to be a hands-on manager. Don't hide in an office - get out there and be there for your team. It's like in football; the head coach who used to play the game commands respect from his team members. Nothing is more annoying than reporting to a boss who knows nothing of what you do on a daily basis.

2. Have Their Backs

Don't throw your team under the bus. Let them know you support them. As a manager, defend your team members. If they aren't performing, give them immediate feedback to correct their problems. Give them opportunities to improve without demoralizing.

3. Be a Filter

Don't get your team caught up in the noise and politics of upper-management. Keep your team focused and on-task. Absorb the drama and only inform your team of important information relevant to their jobs and success.

4. Really CARE About Your Team

It's not about being their best friends; it's about showing a genuine interest in your team members' growth. Take them out to coffee; learn about their aspirations; be an advisor, a mentor…

5. LEAD, Don't "Manage"

Step up your game. Show your team how it's done. Take charge without being pushy or condescending. Someone saw qualities in you to place you in the role you are in today; live up to the expectation and really take ownership. It's all about being accountable to your team and yourself.

Middle management can be a relevant and important role in business today. Be reflective and work on ways to help serve your team. Leading by example will allow the pieces of the organization to fit together (without a "red stapler")!

INDISCRETION #5

The Rebound Relationship

"Look, there is no point in my going out with someone I might really like if I met him at the right time, but who right now has no chance of being anything to me but a transitional man." — Sally

"I'm saying that the right man for you might be out there right now and if you don't grab him, someone else will, and you'll have to spend the rest of your life knowing that someone else is married to your husband." — Marie

In the classic *When Harry Met Sally*, Sally (Meg Ryan) breaks up with her long-time boyfriend, Joe. She discusses her breakup at a brunch with her girlfriends, Marie (Carrie Fisher) and Alice (Lisa Jane Persky). They advise her to not wait too long to get back "out there." However, Sally is hesitant in that she feels the next guy will be nothing more to her than a "transitional man."

In the business world, this isn't any different. When we

spend years in a job and are desperate to find a way out, we end up jumping into a new employment opportunity ("relationship") too quickly. I have seen many cases of people who are at a previous employment for 7-10+ years only to find them "job hopping" for the next 2-3 careers. They were so desperate to "get out" of their stagnant career only to find that the next opportunity was not a long-term fit.

Let's also look at it from the "transitional man" perspective. I read a great blog piece[8] by Andy Porter where he compares his failed recruit to a rebound relationship. He warns that you need to be cautious when recruiting people who may still not be "over" their previous job. There are "warning signs," Porter insists, to keep a lookout for in order to avoid being "burned," such as "the long goodbye" and "still staying friends" with the ex-employer.

So what can be done here? The key is to take a proactive (not reactive) approach to your next career. As a job seeker, if you really want out, be strategic and plan your next move carefully. Lou Adler of the Adler Group wrote a great piece[9] recently that the best time to look for a job is when you already have one. Career growth should be the primary motivator of the change. Also, to avoid the "rebound," make sure you are really done with your former employer. You can't waffle. *Forbes* writer Liz Ryan, CEO of the Human Workplace, writes that there are 5 unmistakable signs that it's time to quit[10]. The common denominator in many of the signs is illness. You have to think of your own physical and mental well being first. If your job is literally making you sick, it surely is time to go!

Be true to yourself; be true to your next employer. As Maya Angelou once said, "Do the best you can until you know better. Then when you know better, do better."

INDISCRETION #6

Recruiters Who Love to Spam

There is a clear disconnect between recruiters and candidates who are in high demand. Recruiters, put yourself in a programmer's shoes: do you honestly believe that a full-time, direct hire employee at Google (who just joined about 8 months prior and has lived/worked in the SF Bay Area his whole career) would want to take a 3-6 month contract job in North Carolina? I smell desperation here... And, imagine what the programmers are saying about these recruiters. Well, it's not good. Alex MacCaw[11], JavaScript programmer and *O'Reilly* author wrote:

"Unfortunately many recruitment emails seem canned at best, automated to spam out to the widest audience possible. It's a wonder these emails work, if indeed they do at all. Looking back through my inbox, here are some of the mistakes I often see recruiters making:

- Canned, with only the name changed
- Asking people to email in their CV or resume

- Not mentioning the company name, only an unspecified 'client'
- Urging you to spam your friends with the opportunity
- Mention ninja, rock stars, or showing a general technical incompetence
- Advertising a job in a country I'm not in, or for a language I don't use.

The problem stems from two very different worlds colliding, one technical, one not—there's no wonder it's a source of friction. Recruiters are trying to hire for jobs that they don't understand, let alone make technical evaluations for."

There needs to be a way in which both the recruiter and the job seeker can meet in the middle. Jim McCoy, VP at ManpowerGroup Solutions, stated in an article for the Society for Human Resource Management[12] that "a one-size-fits-all approach to engaging prospective employees does not work. Organizations should evaluate their talent acquisition strategy and customize job seekers' experiences based on their preferences. Only when employers consider the total value of candidate-centered experiences, will they be able to efficiently and effectively attract and acquire top talent to achieve their business objectives."

McCoy's statement is very true ... and engineers are catching on. Engineer Kevin Owocki wrote a blog piece called "Don't Use Recruiters to Hire Engineers[13]." In the article he states, "[M]ost importantly though, whether you are using a recruiter or not, is to decide what it is you are looking for. This will make your search a whole lot easier.

Determine what makes you happy in terms of technology, projects, customers or product development, salary, etc. This makes it a lot easier to company possible jobs to your requirements and will help you find the right job."

So, recruiters, maybe you should think before you hit send...

INDISCRETION #7

Bad Hiring Begins With Bad Questioning

The talent market is changing. Up and coming talent with bright ideas that can take your company to new heights may get lost in your sea of dull, archaic questioning. A recent article from *FastCompany*[14] points out that as many as 95% of companies admit to recruiting the wrong people each year (based on a Brandon Hall Group survey). The survey showed that 69% of companies pointed towards their "flawed interview process" as having the biggest impact on quality.

The big mistakes that happen in the interview stage are related to the types of questions being asked. Hiring managers fail to properly assess fit through their questioning. Human Workplace CEO and *Forbes* contributor Liz Ryan[15] points out that "great employees who know what they bring to the hiring process can get good jobs with employers who don't treat them like dirt." Ryan states that "traditional" questions such as "Where do you see yourself in five years?" or "What's your greatest weakness?" accomplish nothing. She suggests the following types of questions that dig deeper into one's workplace behavior (and bring a "human touch" to questioning):

- "I can only imagine how busy you are. What got you to come to the interview today — something about our company, or this job, or something else? I'd love to hear about that."
- "When you think about this position what issues spring out as the most critical to address or the greatest learning curves for you?"
- "From the outside, as it were, what do you think our company is doing right and what are we doing wrong?"
- "If we were to come to an agreement and I were to extend a job offer, what would need to be in that job offer in order for you to accept it?"

Entrepreneur[16] magazine released a blog piece called "4 Ways to Test 'Cultural Fit' During the Hiring Process." In it, the author points out that sticking to the "approved list of 10 questions" doesn't accomplish much:

"Interviewees prepare for interviews by rehearsing boilerplate responses to conventional questions. Get a real impression of who they are as people by steering conversations toward unexpected topics. The ability to take the unexpected in stride is a plus, even if their hobbies and interests are different from your own."

In other words, let the interviewee drive the conversation without "prompts or guides." This level of freedom can allow the candidate's personality to shine.

Chances are, your company has experienced bad hiring. It's time to rethink your hiring process. Start by reflecting on your interview questioning. Really take the time to craft questions that will help you understand the whole person. Remember, we are all more than just words on a piece of paper.

INDISCRETION #8

Quiet Time

A friend of mine was once told by her manager that she should "speak up more" for her own career development. Her manager felt that she was too "quiet" in meetings and that she would add much more value to the organization if she would only vocally participate. Is that really good career advice? Are we forced to go outside of our comfort zone to appease the extrovert stereotype?

Susan Cain, the author of *Quiet, The Power of Introverts in a World That Can't Stop Talking*, stated in a July 2012 interview with *Harvard Business Review*[17] that people often assume that being quiet is related to being shy or antisocial; however, it's not that at all. It's about how we respond to stimulation. Lower key situations empower an introvert.

In business, introverts are the great thinkers of an organization. They are the listeners that tend not to generate conflict or unnecessary drama. In fact, they are great in leading teams of extroverts. Extroverts need someone who will take a methodical approach to their high energy and quick reaction. On the flip side, extroverted leaders can help complement the introverted team members, counterbalancing the organization.

It's critical to give introverts their alone time to re-energize. For example, when I was in graduate school, extroverts surrounded me. During breaks, they would ask me if I would go out to lunch with them. As a true introvert, I would turn them down a lot because we spent so much time in class with group projects and social interaction that I needed my alone time during lunch and breaks.

It's time for business leaders and strategists to re-think the value of introverts in organizations. As Susan Cain stated, "If you look at the history of transformative leaders [Eleanor Roosevelt, Gandhi, Rosa Parks] - all these people were quiet and shy. And in a way their power derived from the fact that they weren't about their ego. They were in it purely for their cause. And people can feel that. People can sense it, and that lends them a deep authenticity that is quite priceless."

INDISCRETION #9

Employee Engagement, Interrupted

It's a fact of life: we all get frustrated at work. Even in your dream job, you will have a bad day here and there. My mentor had to remind me that "[we] are all human beings." We sometimes get so caught up in our roles in the company that we forget that small element. When it comes to employee engagement, could it be that simple?

When I was a Yahoo! employee from late 2000 to 2002, I bled purple and yellow. I didn't just work at Yahoo!; it was a lifestyle for me. I found a workplace where I could be myself: I could have a life-sized cutout of Luke Skywalker in my cubicle, and no one would give it a second thought. My needs were met in my role as a Customer Care Tech for Yahoo! GeoCities (remember that service!?). I felt so proud to be part of a well-known brand with a bright future at the time.

Abraham Maslow was a brilliant American psychologist best known for developing the "Hierarchy of Needs." In the hierarchy, there were five levels of needs: physiological, safety, belonging, esteem and self-actualization. The workplace can foster all of these needs; however, belonging and esteem are two particular areas that affect employee engagement.

Belonging is a need that can be satisfied with a solid team environment; a company culture that is inviting, warm, friendly and supportive. The esteem need is the feeling of importance. Fostering an environment that encourages creativity and, in turn, rewards people for hard work and accomplishments satisfies this need.

For example, Kellogg's Corporation[18] operates weekly group "huddles" to communicate news, sales milestones and achievements openly to encourage community. Sue Platt, HR director at Kellogg's stated: "Here at Kellogg's listening is a central premise of the way we work. We believe that our employees have some of the best ideas and that a successful company is one that listens to the grassroots feedback and acts on it. Any employee can raise an issue or a suggestion via their rep who will raise it at one of their monthly meetings."

Let's look at five things your company can do today to foster employee engagement.

1. Have A Common Vision

If you can get your employees to rally around your company's "cause" or "mission," you will have loyal followers. They need to believe in your product. The late Steve Jobs once said in the video "The First Macintosh[19]" that "the greatest people are self-managing — they don't need to be managed. What they need is a common vision, and that's what leadership is — getting consensus around that common vision."

2. Have A Strong Connection With Your Employees

An infographic[20] from Dale Carnegie indicated that 84 percent of how employees feel about their organization is driven by their immediate manager. I highly encourage managers to roll up their sleeves and not hide in an office. They need to model the way and truly care about their team.

3. Create A Family Atmosphere

A case study from PGI[21] indicated that 71 percent of Millennials (Generation Y) want their co-workers to be their second family. It's all about a fun, social atmosphere. My Master's culminating project was a retention study on an IT consulting firm in Silicon Valley. In it, a recurring theme among the people we interviewed was that the employees praised the family atmosphere of the consulting firm. It was like their home away from home.

4. It's The "Little Things" – Appreciation

Research by the Society for Human Resource Management found that 79 percent of those who quit their jobs cite lack of appreciation as the main reason. It's not all about pay raises. Peer recognition and, more importantly, manager recognition are large motivators that can keep the "esteem" need going.

5. Continuous Feedback

As much as we would like to praise people for what they are doing right, we also need to inform people when they are doing something wrong. Immediate and continuous feedback is critical. A Gallup survey of 1,003 US employees in 2009 found that 97 percent of employees weren't engaged when they felt ignored by their managers. Managers need to make time for their employees; a simple 30-minute weekly check-in can do wonders!

INDISCRETION #10

It's Time To Throw Away The Rotten Apples

I have had two careers: HR and Information Technology. One of the best IT jobs I ever held was at Stanford University. I was the in-house tech support person for the Center for Advanced Study in the Behavioral Sciences. Each year, about 40 scholars in the behavioral sciences would take residence at the Center. I would handle their day-to-day IT issues. One year, Robert ("Bob") Sutton was one of our visiting scholars. Bob is a Professor of Management Science and Engineering at Stanford's School of Engineering. At the time, I was heavily focused on IT, so I didn't get involved as much in learning more about his research in organizational behavior.

About 10 years later, however, I began my graduate work in organizational development. I encountered a great piece from Bob in *The Wall Street Journal* entitled "How a Few Bad Apples Ruin Everything[22]." In the article, Bob discusses how we have to find a way to "oust" the bad apples in an organization, no matter how "stellar" the other employees are. There comes a point when the bad ones will drag down the entire organization, so we have to pay close attention to them. We also cannot let the bad employee hold the entire organization hostage and continue to reward the bad behavior.

What Bob reported happens all too often in organizations. Unfortunately, I see it a lot in the consulting industry: the employee has a piss poor attitude; yet, the firm cannot let the person go because "the client loves him." We need to look at the bigger picture. My favorite part of the article was when Bob stated the following:

"But beware: Leaders who believe that destructive superstars are 'too important' to fire often underestimate the damage they can do. Stanford researchers Charles O'Reilly and Jeffrey Pfeffer report a revealing episode at a clothing retailer. The company fired a top-producing salesman who was a bad apple. After he was gone, none of his former colleagues sold as much as he had. But the store's total sales shot up by nearly 30%. The lesson, according to the researchers: 'That one individual brought the others down, and when he was gone, they could do their best.'"

Managers, don't let fear of the unknown cause your organization to suffer. It's time to be bold. As Kevin Gnapoor in the 2004 comedy classic *Mean Girls* said, "Don't let the haters stop you from doing your thang."

ACKNOWLEDGEMENTS & SPECIAL THANKS

Photo Credits

Photos used were purchased through iStock by Getty Images (standard license).

Special Thanks

- My current and former **HR teammates** & the entire **Astreya** family
- **University of California — Santa Cruz, Silicon Valley**'s HR Certificate program: Thanks to the university for allowing me to teach & the students for providing me with inspiration.
- **University of San Francisco**'s Master of Science in Organization Development Class of 2013
- **Starbucks** & **Panera Bread** for providing places to hang out and work on this book

WORKS CITED

Hyperlinks Accessible in Ebook Version

1. Korn, Melissa. "Playing Favorites." *The Wall Street Journal*, August 29, 2011.
2. Swenson, David X. "David McClelland's 3-Need Theory Achievement, Affiliation, Power." Accessed August 30, 2014.
3. Bennis, Warren and Noel Tichy. "Judgment Trumps Experience." *The Wall Street Journal*, November 29, 2007.
4. Drell, Lauren. "Are These the Best Startup Perks You've Ever Seen?" *Mashable*, May 28, 2012.
5. Hayes, Jenny. "5 Ways to be a Useful Middle Manager." *LinkedIn Pulse*, July 29, 2014.
6. Hwang, Victor W. "What's Better for Business: Logic or Emotion? Answers From Neuroscience." *Forbes*, March 27, 2013.
7. "Using Their Own Words, Middle Managers Describe the Nature of Their Jobs." *The Wall Street Journal*, August 6, 2013.

8. Porter, Andy. "5 Signs Your New Hire Is Using You As A Rebound Job." *fistful of talent*, October 6, 2015.
9. Adler, Lou. "The Best Time to Look for a Better Job is When You Already Have One." *LinkedIn Pulse*, August 2, 2016.
10. Ryan, Liz. "Five Unmistakable Signs It's Time To Quit Your Job." *Forbes*, January 30, 2016.
11. Maccaw, Alex. "Alex Maccaw." Accessed July 21, 2015.
12. "Job Candidates Still Seeking Personalized Recruiting Experiences." *SHRM Online*, October 20, 2014.
13. Owocki, Kevin. "Don't Use Recruiters to Hire Engineers." *The World As Perpetual Beta*, July 7, 2015.
14. Dishman, Lydia. "Why Companies Make Bad Hires." *FastCompany*, September 1, 2015.
15. Ryan, Liz. "You Won't Hire Great People Asking These Stupid Interview Questions." *Forbes*, August 24, 2015.
16. Tantry, Sathvik. "4 Ways to Test 'Cultural Fit' During the Hiring Process." *Entrepreneur*, September 3, 2015.
17. "The Power of the Introvert in Your Office." *Harvard Business Review*, July 2012.
18. "Building a Better Workplace Through Motivation." *Business Case Studies*. Accessed October 10, 2013.
19. "Steve Jobs in a documentary about Apple (1985)," YouTube video, 10:38, documentary about

Apple and Steve Jobs, posted by "EverySteveJobs-Video," September, 23, 2014.

20. "How to Engage Employees by Fostering Positive Emotions." *Dale Carnegie*. Accessed October 10, 2013.

21. "When It Comes to Business, Does Father Still Know Best?" *HR Bartender*, August 2013.

22. Sutton, Robert. "How a Few Bad Apples Ruin Everything." *The Wall Street Journal*, October 24, 2011.

CLASSIC BONUS ARTICLES

For the hardcover edition (updated March 2025), I am including additional published business articles that I have written over the years. I hope to create an updated version of this entire book once I complete my Doctoral degree in May 2028. You can visit **bluemilk.co** to find the original articles with hyperlinks to the sources/references. Enjoy!

CLASSIC BONUS ARTICLE #1

Can You Save Your Employees Before They Begin a New Job Search?

> *"For all of my career, I've been trying to catch people after they do something horrible. For once in my life, I'd like to catch somebody BEFORE they do something horrible, all right? Can you understand that?"* - ATF Agent Doug Carlin (*Déjà Vu*, 2006)

One of my favorite time travel movies is *Déjà Vu* from 2006. In it, Denzel Washington plays ATF Agent Doug Carlin. He works with a team of scientists and travels back into the past to prevent a disaster from happening on a ferry in New Orleans. I think we all would love to travel back in time to stop something bad from happening. In business, losing a key employee when you could have prevented it can be tragic as well. It can cost, on average, some $3,341 to hire a new employee, according to the Society for Human Resource Management. This is why companies are investing in predictive analytics to help salvage their employees.

According to an article from *Entrepreneur Magazine*, in

the third quarter of 2014, 47% of employees felt confident that they would find a new position in the next six months that would be fitting for their experience level. This is up 11 percentage points from four years ago. In addition to a strong job search market, there are some clear behavioral signs that employees may be looking:

- Coming in chronically late or early
- Becoming less friendly / more agitated with colleagues / employee engagement
- Completing a new degree / certification
- A major life event, such as divorce or marriage
- Significant company restructuring / changes

With all these predictors, it's no wonder that data scientists are now creating algorithms to help companies turn these warning signs into a true predictive science. In March 2015, *The Wall Street Journal* reported that data scientists are creating models to help predict which workers might leave first. They refine variables depending on which are the most predictive given a specific company or specific group in an organization. According to the article, "VoloMetrix Inc., which examines HR data as well as anonymized employee email and calendar data, found that it could predict flight risk up to a year in advance for employees who were spending less time interacting with certain colleagues or attending events beyond required meetings. And Ultimate Software found a correlation between a client's employees who waived their benefits coverage and those who left the company."

Keep in mind that predictors are fine and dandy, but,

without action on the part of the company, they are useless. If it's found that John Doe is slated to resign in 6 months if there is no opportunity for advancement, then the company needs to find a way to advance John within the company. It's not easy; there are times when a company cannot help their employees because there are genuinely no opportunities. Communication between managers and their direct reports becomes very critical.

We may not be able to go back in time like Denzel Washington, but a combination of predictive analytics and true organizational leadership may be the step in the right direction to save your employees.

CLASSIC BONUS ARTICLE #2

Everything I Need To Know About Employee Referrals I Learned From Watching

I recently attended **Star Wars Celebration** at the ExCeL Exhibition Center in London. One of the highlights of Day 1 was a fan screening of ***Star Wars: Episode IV - A New Hope***. What's always fun about fan screenings is that you are surrounded by a passionate group of people who really get into the story, even though they have seen the movie hundreds of times. Being a staffing industry professional, when I watched this time, I wanted to see if I could find some HR-related themes in the film.

When we reached the scene where we first meet Luke Skywalker, he and his uncle, Owen Lars, agree to purchase droids from a group of scavengers, the Jawas. The Jawas, essentially, act as members of a staffing company who "pitch" their "candidates" (droids) to Luke and Owen. The two droids that we meet early in the movie, C-3PO and R2-D2, are among those up for sale. Owen, unfortunately, decides to pass on R2-D2 in favor of R5-D4, another astromech droid. He then proceeds to "interview" C-3PO on the spot:

> **Uncle Owen**: *You, I suppose you're programmed for etiquette and protocol.*
> **C-3PO**: *Protocol? Why, it's my primary function, sir. I am well-versed in all the customs.*
> **Uncle Owen**: *I have no need for a protocol droid.*
> **C-3PO**: *Of course you haven't, sir. Not in an environment such as this. That is why I have been programmed...*
> **Uncle Owen**: *What I really need is a droid who understands the binary language of moisture vaporators.*
> **C-3PO**: *Vaporators? Sir, my first job was programing binary load lifters; very similar to your vaporators in most respects.*
> **Uncle Owen**: *Can you speak Bocce?*
> **C-3PO**: *Of course I can, sir. It's like a second language to me...*
> **Uncle Owen**: *Yeah, alright. Shut up. I'll take this one.*
> **C-3PO**: *Shutting up, Sir.*

C-3PO, who does a great job of selling himself to Owen, is now "employed." However, his friend and colleague, R2-D2, is not selected. On their way to being cleaned up, R5-D4's motivator gives out which gives C-3PO the perfect opportunity to refer his former colleague.

> **R5-D4**: *(blows its motivator)*
> **Luke**: *Uncle Owen!*
> **Uncle Owen**: *Yeah?*
> **Luke**: *This R2 unit has a bad motivator. Look!*

Uncle Owen: Hey, what are you trying to push on us?
Jawa: (Speaking alien language defensively)
C-3PO: [Referring to R2-D2] Excuse me, Sir, but that R2 unit is in prime condition, a real bargain.
Luke: Uncle Owen!
Uncle Owen: Yeah?
Luke: What about that one?
Uncle Owen: What about that blue one? We'll take that one.
Jawa: (Speaking alien language)
Luke: [Referring to R5-D4] Yeah, take this away.
C-3PO: I'm quite sure you'll be very pleased with that one, sir. He really is in first-class condition. I've worked with him before. Here he comes.
Luke: Okay, let's go.
C-3PO: [Speaking to R2-D2] Now, don't you forget this. Why I should stick my neck out for you is quite beyond my capacity.

So, essentially, R5-D4 was a "bad hire" on Uncle Owen's part, and now a trusted colleague in R2-D2 can help the Lars family at their moisture farm. Of course, as we know, R2-D2 had other intentions: find Obi-Wan Kenobi and deliver the information on how to destroy the dreaded DEATH STAR to the Rebellion. If C-3PO did not refer R2, Luke Skywalker may have never become a Jedi and the Star Wars universe would have been in complete peril.

Star Wars is just a movie, of course, so let's look at this in real life. Employee referrals are critical. According to a recent SHRM article, employee referral programs continue to be viewed as a key source of quality hires—ranked third, at 32 percent, by LinkedIn users, behind social professional networks (43 percent) and online job boards (42 percent). Referred employees tend to integrate into the organization faster, have a longer tenure and perform better. Referrals are ranked as one of the "three most essential and long-lasting trends in recruiting." So, keep building out your employee referral programs. You never know; you could save the galaxy!

CLASSIC BONUS ARTICLE #3

Can't Find A Job? Become A 'Liberal Arts Techie'

"I have decided that this is the year I am getting married," declared Charlotte York on the HBO series *Sex and the City*. Desperate to be a wife, Charlotte found solace within a fictitious book called *Marriage, Incorporated: How to Apply Successful Business Strategies to Finding a Husband*. In it, she learned that she shouldn't be spending so much time with her "dysfunctional single women" friends, but, instead, she should spend time with her married friends. Bachelor friends of married men were New York's "best untapped resource," per Charlotte. In other words, Charlotte sought nontraditional means to find her perfect "candidate" essentially, taking the law into her own hands to find her soul mate.

What does this mean when it comes to finding a job? Competition is fierce. In particular, people who have a more "generic" skill set (i.e., a liberal arts background and little specialized skills) have a difficult time differentiating themselves. They have to get creative, like Charlotte from

Sex and the City. A recent blog post from *The Wall Street Journal* entitled "Have Liberal Arts Degree, Will Code" points out that liberal arts majors are turning "techie" by developing coding skills. One Duke University English and Theater studies grad found herself with a new career that earned $20,000 more per year after acquiring frontend web development skills.

It's not a foreign concept to marry the liberal arts with technology. Apple co-founder, the late Steve Jobs, once stated in a 1996 NPR interview that "[I] think our major contribution [to computing] was in bringing a liberal arts point of view to the use of computers. If you really look at the ease of use of the Macintosh, the driving motivation behind that was to bring not only ease of use to people … but it was to bring beautiful fonts and typography to people, it was to bring graphics to people… so that they could see beautiful photographs, or pictures, or artwork, et cetera… to help them communicate."

So what are some technical careers that can be enjoyed by people with liberal arts degrees? "Technical" careers are broad these days. For example, my sister works for Wells Fargo. They are such a huge company that their Human Resources department has its own marketing communications team. She helps build and push out HR-related content to their company Intranet. Some HTML she learned as a hobbyist back in 1996, when she was an undergrad majoring in Sociology, gave her the foundation to understand tools such as Dreamweaver and MS SharePoint. She has no formal tech training; just a passion to learn and adapt to new technology quickly.

The point here is to take control of your career. There

are skills in high demand out there, and you don't have to have a Computer Science degree from Stanford to acquire them. Channel your inner Charlotte York: declare that this is the year you will find your dream job, and make it happen (just don't break too many hearts along the way…).

CLASSIC BONUS ARTICLE #4

5 Bad Habits Can Threaten Your Company's Cyber Security

To: Jane Doe jdoe@ajax-corp.com>
From: John Smith jsmith@ajax-corp.com>

Jane,

Process a payment of $20,000 to the account information attached. Code to admin expenses and let me know when completed.

Thanks.
John Smith
CEO
AJAX Corporation
San Jose, CA USA

The above sample email may seem like a legitimate email from a company's top executive; however, this email is actually a scam. A scammer emails an employee and pretends to be the CEO, boss or other person in charge. The person will ask for a certain amount to be transferred to an imaginary supplier. This scam, also known as BEC ("Business Email Compromise"), is a growing financial fraud that has resulted in actual and attempted losses of more than a billion dollars to businesses worldwide. The FBI reports that "since the FBI's Internet Crime Complaint Center (IC3) began tracking BEC scams in late 2013, it has compiled statistics on more than 7,000 U.S. companies that have been victimized—with total dollar losses exceeding $740 million. That doesn't include victims outside the U.S. and unreported losses."

With threats like BEC, companies need to invest in the education of their employees on cybersecurity. According to a new study by the Computing Technology Industry Association (CompTIA), 45% of employees receive no cybersecurity training from their employers. Other key findings include the following:

- 63% of employees use their work mobile device for personal activities.
- 94% of employees connect their laptop/mobile to public Wi-Fi networks.
- 49% of employees have at least 10 logins, but only 34% have at least 10 unique logins.

The lack of cyber security training is something that HR, IT and business leaders need to take seriously in an effort to protect company data. It will involve not only general best practices training but also shaping user behavior.

To give you a head start in developing an IT security training program, I have listed 5 key areas of focus and tips to help educate your users to change their "bad habits."

Bad Habit #1: Connecting to Public Wi-Fi Networks

The availability of free, public Wi-Fi is both a blessing and a curse for working professionals. Being able to stay connected in the digital age is critical for both personal and business communication. However, open public networks provide little buffer between the end user and potential threats. Learning how to protect oneself ensures important business data remains safe. Internet Security company ZoneAlarm recommends the following security measures:

Choose your network wisely

"Using your wits can help you choose a relatively safe network and avoid hackers. One common hacking technique is known as a man-in-the-middle attack. In this type of attack, a hacker creates a nefarious network alongside an authentic network that's being offered by a legitimate establishment. If you use the hacker's network instead of the legitimate one, all your information is channeled directly via the hacker's network, providing the hacker easy access to your information. To avoid using a hacker's site, double check with the concierge/waiter/librarian of the establishment offering you free Wi-Fi to make sure you choose the right network. If you see two networks with strangely similar names, let the establishment know, as one of these networks could well be a hacker's trap."

Close shared folders on your laptop

"Using shared folders can be really handy when you're working in an office network, but as soon as your computer is open to public Wi-Fi, your shared folders can be viewed by anyone who is on the network. You can't possibly know all the people who are accessing that free network, and even if you could, you probably don't want all your shared files open to them. To prevent this from happening, change the file sharing settings on your laptop, and make sure that privacy settings are different for public and private networks."

Turn off automatic Wi-Fi connections

"Public Wi-Fi is great, but there is no reason to open your device to it all day and all night. Consider it akin to the front door of your home. You want to be able to open and close the door when you go in and out of your home, but you certainly don't need to leave the door open in the middle of the night, or while you're taking a shower or watching TV. So why leave your mobile device open to public Wi-Fi when you're not using it? All it takes is a tap or two to turn your automatic Wi-Fi connection on and off. So if you don't plan on using public W-iFi while you're out and about, leave the connection closed."

Use a VPN service

"Using a VPN protects your privacy by ensuring that all your online activities remain private. So if someone is trying to track your online activities, your tracks only lead to the VPN. Everything else that you do online is untrackable. The use of VPNs is increasingly common on desktop computers, as people realize the importance of protecting their privacy online. Mobile device-oriented VPNs such as ZoneAlarm Capsule provide you with a similar level of privacy on your mobile device, making sure that both outgoing and incoming communications are private and safe."

Bad Habit #2: Responding to Scammers

As I mentioned in the beginning of this blog piece, BECs are very common. Your organization can lose millions of dollars if your staff is not trained properly to identify the warning signs of a malicious BEC. The FBI advises on the following:

- Verify changes in vendor payment location and confirm requests for transfer of funds.
- Be wary of free, web-based email accounts, which are more susceptible to being hacked.

- Be careful when posting financial and personnel information to social media and company websites.
- Regarding wire transfer payments, be suspicious of requests for secrecy or pressure to take action quickly.
- Consider financial security procedures that include a two-step verification process for wire transfer payments.
- Create intrusion detection system rules that flag emails with extensions that are similar to company e-mail but not exactly the same. For example, .co instead of .com.
- If possible, register all Internet domains that are slightly different than the actual company domain.
- Know the habits of your customers, including the reason, detail, and amount of payments. Beware of any significant changes.

Bad Habit #3: Using Random Portable Storage Devices

CompTIA mentions in their study that, despite the prevalence of free cloud storage and the convenience of email, 58% of those surveyed rely on USB-based storage drives to transfer files across devices. There are many problems with using portable storage to store company data (in addition to the obvious one: losing the device!). According to the study, around 35% have borrowed someone else's USB stick to copy or transfer a file, while 22% of employees would hypothetically pick up a USB stick they found in public. Of that group, 84% would go so far as to plug the USB into one of their own devices.

Obviously, there is no stopping people from using portable storage. However, we can educate ourselves to become more savvy in protecting data. Norton by Symantec suggests the following ways to protect portable drive data:

Protect your data. Avoid copying sensitive personal data such as your Social Security, credit card or bank account information on a USB device.

Use encryption. If you absolutely must put sensitive information on a USB device, encrypt it first. Well-known encryption programs like PGP can be downloaded from reliable websites and used to encode information so it can't be viewed without being decoded first, according to Siciliano, the Boston security expert.

Use secure devices. Some newer model USB drives have safety features such as fingerprint authentication that protect data from would-be hackers. Other devices have built-in encryption which eliminates the need to use a separate software program to scramble your information, according to Siciliano.

Pick a storage spot. Because USB drives are so small they're easy to misplace. Pick a spot on your kitchen counter, dresser or desk and make it your designated USB drive drop spot so you'll always know where to look for them. Or use the lanyards that come on some devices to hang them up with your car keys.

Keep home, office devices separate. Don't use the same flash drives for home and work to avoid accidentally introducing a virus you picked up from an infected device into your company's office network. Most businesses have policies about what can be plugged into the company network, so if you ever do work from home, it's advisable to acquaint yourself with your company's rules, says Scudder, the New York security consultant.

Bad Habit #4: Sharing Too Much Information on Social Media

A number of people I know with governmental Top Security Clearances aren't even allowed to have a Facebook page. It seems a little extreme, but, in fact, it's not. Social media is an easy way for hackers and those with malicious intent to grab information about you and your company.

The University of Pennsylvania's Offices of Information Systems & Computing and Audit, Compliance & Privacy posted the following considerations:

Private postings can often easily be made public. Even if you allow only a small number of contacts to see your post, those contacts may have privacy settings that allow sharing of your content with an undefined set of their contacts. Additionally, any recipient of your post can take action to copy your content and trigger "viral" spreading thanks to the speed and power of Internet sharing.

Some information should not be posted. Don't share personal, confidential or otherwise sensitive information on social media if it could cause harm to an individual or individuals. Some information, such as health, financial and other highly personal information, is almost always sensitive. Also, posting your own location and even the location of people you know can be a dangerous practice for victims of harassment or stalking, burglary or people with other privacy concerns.

Some information may lead to "spear phishing." You may share information about yourself that may not seem to be sensitive (e.g., birthday, job title, education, names of friends and relatives, likes and dislikes, or favorite charities), but phishing scammers may piece this information together and use it to send you an email that contains information or appears from an individual or business that would make you think that it is legitimate. This is known as "spear phishing." The email may cause you to provide password information or click on a link or attachment that contains malware.

Bad Habit #5: Poor Password Choices

There are so many logins and passwords to keep up with that it is not surprising that some personal passwords are also passwords used in business. Although technology such as two-factor authentication can be used to tighten security, the CompTIA study points out that 41% of workers are not familiar with two-factor authentication, and 27% are familiar with the name but don't understand the concept. Less than half (48%) voluntarily apply two-factor authentication to their accounts. What else can be done, then, to strengthen passwords?

A recent article from *Fast Company* uncovered a new technique for password strengthening. Applied security researcher Dr. Markus Jakobsson's technique called "fastwords" ties together storytelling, password strength and probability. Cracking of a phrase over 10 to 12 characters cannot be done effectively through brute force, so crackers would need to try word combinations and other techniques. Therefore, the improbability of the combination of three words in that order becomes paramount.

It's imperative that companies work harder to train their employees to protect themselves against the dangers that exist in our technology-driven society. The more we educate ourselves, the less likely we can be vulnerable professionally and personally.

CLASSIC BONUS ARTICLE #5

Mining for Talent: Organizational "Hidden Gems"

This past summer, I visited Virginia City, Nevada, a historic mining community that was once one of the richest locations in the world. Today, Virginia City is a great tourist spot and was recently made famous for its haunted locations. In my visit, I came upon Chollar Mine, where miners blasted and carted out some $17 million in gold and silver over the course of its history.

When it became a historical monument, the mining stopped; however, the tour guide explained that close to 70% of the resources (gold/silver) remain untapped. That's huge! So, it got me to thinking about organizations. Are there "hidden gems" that you have ignored? What has stopped you from mining for talent?

Taking a Risk When Recruiting

Several years ago, I recruited entry-level desktop

support talent. I wanted to do something different from hiring "cookie cutter" techs. I wanted bright, "liberal arts techie"-types, as I found that they made the best technicians. Why? Well, although they didn't have the certs, they were college educated (BA/BS degree), excelled in communication and had a passion for technology. With that in mind, I came across a resume on Craigslist of a recent graduate from Spelman College. She was a robotics champion at her school. She had no direct tech support experience, but she did have a BS in Computer Science. So, when I met her, I sensed that she was really bright and could pick things up quickly. Needless to say, the traditional recruiter would have passed on her because she didn't have any direct experience or industry certifications. Sure enough, today she is a lead support engineer at a major Silicon Valley company. I took a risk that paid off in the end.

Succession Planning Through People Analytics

As I mentioned in a previous blog piece, data scientists are creating models to help predict which workers might leave first. The "people analytics" market, as they are now calling it, is combining traditional HR data with real-world business issues in order to build out programs that drive employee engagement, retention and satisfaction. Through the data, we can uncover hidden gems in the talent pool that may have been overlooked. As *Forbes* contributor Josh Bersin points out:

- High tech companies now know why top

engineers quit and how to build compensation and work environments to get people to stay.
- Financial services companies are now analyzing why certain people commit fraud and what environmental or hiring issues might contribute to such violations.
- Product companies are now analyzing the demographic, educational and experiential factors that correlate with high performing sales people and why top sales people quit.
- Health care companies are looking at why certain hospitals or departments have higher infection rates and what people issues are behind these problems.
- Manufacturers and product companies are looking at the patterns of email traffic and communications to understand how high performing managers behave and what work styles result in the highest levels of performance.

Losing Touch With High Potentials

HBR's classic piece called "How to Keep Your Top Talent" discusses 6 critical mistakes that firms make when they assume too much about their high potential / top talent pool. Mistake #6 points out the dangers of failing to link top talent with the company's corporate strategy.

"A firm's most talented staffers can have meaningful effects across the business. But when burgeoning talent is misidentified, unchallenged, or unrewarded, these individuals become a drag on overall performance. Even worse, their disengagement and eventual derailment can lead to depleted leadership ranks and damage employee commitment and retention across the firm."

This is why it's critical that organizational leaders maintain a proper pulse check on their existing staff to retain and unlock potential that may have otherwise gone unnoticed.

CLASSIC BONUS ARTICLE #6

Employee Engagement is More Than a Cause – It's a Mission!

I am a big fan of Post-It Notes (the kind from 3M Corporation — not the generic "Office Depot" brand, mind you). I am so much a fan that I say to people that I would be happy just being a janitor at 3M Corporation so I can be in the presence of their latest innovations...

That may sound a little quirky, and maybe a bit crazy, but the point is that I believe in their product so much that I would take any job opportunity just to be a part of the organization. As an employer, wouldn't you like to have employees who bleed for your company? As a candidate, wouldn't you like to find a job where you walk into work each day smiling and become the biggest cheerleader of the organization?

This is what employee engagement is all about... and it starts with a mission.

If you can get your employees to rally around your company's "mission," you will have loyal followers. They need to believe in your product. The late Steve Jobs once said in the video "The First Macintosh" that "the greatest people are self-managing — they don't need to be managed. What they need is a common vision, and that's what leadership is — getting consensus around that common vision."

Having a mission gives a sense of purpose to an organization. We can tie this back to the work of Abraham Maslow and his "Hierarchy of Needs." In the hierarchy, there were five levels of needs: physiological, safety, belonging, esteem and self-actualization. The workplace can foster all of these needs; however, belonging and esteem are two particular areas that affect employee engagement. Belonging is a need that can be satisfied with a solid team environment; a company culture that is inviting, warm, friendly and supportive. The esteem need is the feeling of importance. Fostering an environment that encourages creativity and, in turn, rewards people for hard work and accomplishments satisfies this need.

Gallup released an article in March of 2014 that emphasized the importance of the company mission. Here are some key highlights from the article:

Mission drives loyalty across generations.

Understanding a company's purpose helps employees answer yes to the question "Do I belong here?" Gallup's research shows that ensuring employees have opportunities to do what they do best every day and emphasizing mission and purpose are the two strongest factors for retaining Millennials, Generation X-ers, and Baby Boomers. More than one in four Millennials strongly agree with the statement: "If the job market improves in the next 12 months, I will look for a job with a different organization." This makes it more important than ever to focus on strengths and mission to drive down the cost of turnover and prevent the loss of key employees, especially among Millennials.

Mission fosters customer engagement.

A strong mission promotes brand differentiation, consumer passion, and brand engagement. Unfortunately, only about four in 10 employees (41%) know what their company stands for and what makes its brand different from its competitors'. This lack of brand awareness is not a marketing problem; it is a mission-driven leadership and management problem.

Mission can be measured.

To maximize the value of mission and purpose, leaders need a reliable assessment of employees' attitudes about their work and how it connects with the company's purpose, such as their responses to the "mission and purpose" item in Gallup's Q12 employee engagement survey. Leaders and managers should use this information to guide them as they tackle the challenge of helping employees connect their work behaviors to the company's ultimate purpose.

People want to build a career in a company they believe

in. It's pretty clear that having a mission or sense of purpose that people can rally around is essential in employee engagement. Whether you are a small company developing your first mission statement or an established company that is looking to rebrand yourself, it's time to find your purpose and lead with it!

CLASSIC BONUS ARTICLE #7

Think Different — Keys to Managing a Successful Generation Y Team

In one of my graduate courses, we watched the short documentary called "The First Macintosh." In it, a young Steve Jobs revealed managerial secrets that aided in the success of Apple at the time. He hired bright, fresh talent that weren't the seasoned pro's of the day... they were just good, smart people with a common vision and passion. The quote that resonated most for me was the following:

> "The greatest people are self managing — they don't need to be managed. What they need is a common vision, and that's what leadership is...getting a consensus around that common vision."

What's interesting is that the people in this video are now the parents of Generation Y, who are starting to dominate today's workforce. Like the members of Steve's Macintosh team, today's Gen Y workforce thrives in a similar environment — an environment in which creativity and laissez faire management run amuck.

Recently, I surveyed my team (primarily filled with Gen Y talent) and asked them why they liked working for our company (a rapidly growing, late stage start-up in the heart of Silicon Valley). Here are some of their responses:

- A competitive but supportive atmosphere
- Advancement opportunities
- Work hard, play hard with strong accountability from management
- Little to no micro-management
- Teamwork with shared goals
- Open, fun company with a family atmosphere
- Recognition for hard work
- Change and innovation

Tons of articles have been written on how to manage this new workforce. As you can see, they just want an open, collaborative environment and be surrounded by co-workers with a common vision under the guidance of management that are hands-off, yet keep them accountable. Going back to the "First Macintosh," Steve Jobs acted as what they called "the new manager" — the "head coach," if you will, who led the team while allowing them to have the creative freedom necessary to innovate.

There is a secret sauce to managing the new generation — you just have to "Think Different."

CLASSIC BONUS ARTICLE #8

Are We Ready For a World Without Managers?

"If everyone had to think outside the box, maybe it was the box that needed fixing." — Malcom Gladwell, *What the Dog Saw*

In 2013, online retailer Zappos announced that it would transition away from a traditional management structure to a less hierarchical, manager-free system called Holacracy. Holacracy is the brainchild of Brian Robertson and his software company Ternary Software. Power is distributed away from traditional managers in a Holacracy model and given back to the employees; however, they are given a clear set of rules and expectations. In a Holacracy, there is still organizational structure, but it's radically different from the traditional organization.

The transition to Holacracy is now a reality at Zappos. CEO Tony Hsieh announced in a memo that, as of April

30, 2015, "people manager" positions at Zappos would be eliminated. Employees were given until then to accept the new system or take a buyout. According to the *Las Vegas Sun*, over 200 employees have accepted buyouts offered by the company. This amounted to about 14 percent of the company's workforce.

Is this an emerging trend? Are we at the point where we need to radically "think outside the box" to fix organizations?

The Managerless Organization

The Holacracy website outlines how the traditional company works versus a "Holacratic" organization:

Traditional Companies	With Holacracy
Job Descriptions: Each person has exactly one job. Job descriptions are imprecise, rarely updated and often irrelevant.	**Roles**: Roles are defined around the work, not people, and are updated regularly. People fill several roles.
Delegated Authority: Managers loosely delegate authority. Ultimately, their decision always trumps.	**Distributed Authority**: Authority is truly distributed to teams and roles. Decisions are made locally.
Big Re-Orgs: The org structure is rarely revisited, mandated from the top.	**Rapid Interactions**: The org structure is regularly updated via small iterations. Every team self-organizes.
Office Politics: Implicit rules slow down change and favor people "in the know."	**Transparent Rules**: Everyone is bound by the same rules, CEO included. Rules are visible to all.

If you look at these general concepts, it really doesn't seem too bad. No office politics? People actually performing the work have decision-making power? Real accountability even at the CEO-level? This all sounds too good to be true, right?

Here are some examples of companies that have successfully adopted Holacracy and how they are getting by:

Valve Software is a video gaming company that has been around since 1996. According to *Fast Company*, they forgo titles and managers altogether and have the most extreme form of Holacracy. Check out their quirky (yet entertaining) company handbook. You shouldn't expect any less from a video gaming company.

Medium, a blog-publishing platform founded by Twitter co-founders Evan Williams and Biz Stone, adopted the following tenants from Holacracy:

- No people managers. Maximum autonomy.
- Organic expansion. When a job gets too big, hire another person.
- Tension resolution. Identify issues people are facing, write them down, and resolve them systematically.
- Make everything explicit—from vacation policies to decision makers in each area.
- Distribute decision-making power and discourage consensus seeking.
- Eliminate all the extraneous factors that worry people so they can focus on work.

And, of course, we know now that Zappos is fully moving forward with the managerless system.

Can this model work for everyone? Is this the one-size-fits all solution that we have been waiting for?

The Common Denominator

The late Steve Jobs once said in the documentary "The First Macintosh" that "the greatest people are self managing - they don't need to be managed. What they need is a common vision, and that's what leadership is...getting a consensus around that common vision."

Start-ups and smaller organizations tend to have to "think different" in order to succeed. Decisions have to be quick; employees have to be dedicated and work long hours; and employees are more involved and generally have to wear many hats. The sense of loyalty and commitment comes from having a common vision. When an organization is "flat," it becomes clearer what the goals are, who is accountable and so forth. Therefore, a full Holacracy can most likely be achieved in a smaller organizations, technical organizations (where creative autonomy and Scrum models of project management are very popular) or start-ups.

So what about larger organizations? Jacob Morgan, the author of *The Future of Work*, has studied the Holacracy phenomena in depth. In his research, most companies are attempting to find ways to "flatten" their organizations; however, going completely managerless isn't their solution. Morgan notes that "organizations such as Tangerine (formerly ING Direct Canada) do have managers yet they don't focus on these titles or roles internally. Other companies like Whirlpool have also shifted away from traditional managerial roles by creating four different types of 'leadership,' where everyone at the company is considered a leader of some kind (for example if you are an entry level or junior employee you may be called 'a leader of self.')."

The Future of Work

As David Allen, author of *Getting Things Done* and a

business leader with years of Holacracy experience in his own company, stated that Holacracy "is not a panacea: it won't resolve all of an organization's tensions and dilemmas. But, in my experience, it does provide the most stable ground from which to recognize, frame, and address them."

Holacracy is obviously not going to work for every organization. However, given the adoption of all or part of the model by many organizations, it's pretty clear that traditional approaches to work are dramatically changing. Most companies will not be able eliminate managers completely, but they can work to reduce the need for micromanagement. In turn, employees can become more autonomous and greater creativity and productivity can resume.

ABOUT THE AUTHOR

Jenny (Hayes) Carhart, **MSOD**, **PHR**, has over 20 years of experience in the staffing and technology industries. She earned her BA in Psychology with Academic Distinction from the University of Oklahoma and her MS in Organization Development from the University of San Francisco. A certified Professional in Human Resources from HRCI, Jenny is currently working towards her Doctorate in Business Administration at the University of South Florida's Muma College of Business. She resides in San Jose, California with her husband (Allan), stepsons (Chris & Henry), and cats.

linkedin.com/in/cabbagejenny

ABOUT BLUE MILK PUBLISHING

Blue Milk Publishing represents independent authors of both fiction and non-fiction works.

Please visit **bluemilk.co** for more information.

Non-Fiction

The Cheating Boyfriend (And Other Organizational Indiscretions) (January 2017) by Jenny (Hayes) Carhart, MSOD, PHR

Fiction

Things That Go Bump in the Night, Volume One: Urban Legends (October 2023) by JC Bratton

Project Impossible: Complete Edition (October 2024) by Henry Carhart